Tuesday – Sunday, 11am – 8pm
T +44 (0)20 7921 0943
F +44 (0)20 7921 0607
poetrylibrary.org.uk

Level 5 at Royal Festival Hall
Southbank Centre, Belvedere Road
London SE1 8XX

Books may be renewed by telephone

POETRY LIBRARY

The Saison Poetry Library housing
the Arts Council Poetry Collection at

SOUTHBANK CENTRE

Supported by
ARTS COUNCIL
ENGLAND

D1513042

Almost Memories

Tim Cunningham

A REVIVAL POETRY BOOK

Revival Press

Limerick – Ireland

Copyright © Tim Cunningham 2014

First Published in Ireland by
Revival Press
Limerick Ireland

Revival Press is the poetry imprint of
The Limerick Writers' Centre
12 Barrington Street, Limerick, Ireland

www.limerickwriterscentre.com
www.facebook.com/limerickwriterscentre

Tim Cunningham
e-mail: catnamaste@aol.com
www.timcunninghampoetry.co.uk

Cover Image: 'Heron' by Eamonn McCarthy
Cover Design: Dania Fernández Fernández
Book Design: Dania Fernández Fernández

ISBN: 978-0-9928625-5-8

A CIP catalogue number for this publication is available from The British Library

We acknowledge the support of:

For John O'Doherty,
Brian McLaughlin and Pete Suttle.

By the same author:

Don Marcelino's Daughter

Unequal Thirds

Kyrie

Siege

ACKNOWLEDGEMENTS

are due to the editors of the following magazines, etc., in which some of these poems have appeared or been accepted for publication:

Acumen
Cyphers
The Frogmore Papers
The Interpreter's House
Lapidus
Orbis
Revival Literary Journal
The Shop
The Stony Thursday Book

and the anthologies:

The Book of Love and Loss, Belgrave Press (2014)
From the City to the Saltings: Poems from Essex, Poetry in Practice (2013)
The Limerick Poetry Anthology (2014), Astrolabe Press

Special thanks for the award of a Patrick and Katherine Kavanagh Fellowship, which helped to make this selection possible.

Contents

Almost Memories 10

Ghost Ship 11

In My Father's House 13

A Sandstone Rock 16

Among the Rhododendrons 17

Riverbank 18

Local Anaesthetic 19

Seven Wonders of the Parish 20

Lady River 21

Sunset on the Shannon 22

Forecast 23

Sidewinder 24

Zebra Finch 25

Not Being There 26

Losing His Grip 27

A Seasonal Migration 28

Changing Their Tune 29

A Candle in the Window 30

A Prayer in Search of Its God 31

Maleficium 32

The Minus Decibels 33

Horae Canonicae 34

Her Christmas Card List 37

Taking Down the Decorations 38

Raspberry Ripple 39

Watching Agatha What'shername 40

The Invisible Man 42

Allegro 43

Jigsaw Man 44

The Final Credits 45

Drawn Thread Embroidery 46

The Everyday Aesthetic 47

This Hillside Rock 48

Bard 50

The Salon of the Refused 51

Harp 52

Lifebuoy 54

Interrupting Children's Hour 55

Last Minute Packing 56

Counting the Seconds 57

Sundial 58

The Landlord's Daughter 59

1888 60

Proclamations, 1916 62

In the Valley of the Thrushes 63

Almost Memories

I remember silver thistles
On his regimental badge,
Bright as the *silvoed* star.
Like pay book and New Testament,
It came with his effects.

As to our sun-forged summers
On the riverbank, patiently
Waiting with bamboo rods
Or skimming stones towards
The rushes on the opposite bank,

Holding his gloved hand,
Admiring, through snowflakes,
The train set in Todd's window
With the track that we would lay
By the forest of the Christmas tree,

Blowing out six candles
On the birthday cake
When he came home for tea
And racing him to the last
Of the musical chairs . . .

These, like searching for the ball
In the tall grass and thistles,
Are also dead stars
In the constellation
Of almost memories.

Ghost Ship

My mother kept his memory bottled up
As if it were a vintage for herself
Alone. So, like hot tea from a saucer,
I sipped away at absence, slurped clues
From photos standing to attention
On the wall or on the dresser at their ease,
From citations I could not understand,
The *silvoed* Cameronian badge she kept
Pinned on her bag or favourite fawn coat
And, mostly, from the clipper in the bottle.

Long, slim and graceful with three tall masts
And a fair wind billowing her sails,
The ship sailed west on the polished sideboard
Between the wedding photograph and the fresh
War grave. In the wedding shot, she wore
A hat like the one that clouded Bergman's face
In 'Casablanca'. He wore a three-piece suit
And patent leather shoes. They both wore rings,
Symbols of a lasting love cut short
By the ring on a World War Two grenade.

The clipper never faced a fierce sou'wes'ter
But the lookout in the crow's nest spied her
Through the bottle she dusted every day,
Watched her keep the rented room shipshape,
Mop the floor as if swamping out some deck
Or, at six o'clock precisely, fix places
For the children's tea, fit for a captain's table.
Anchored by love, she spent nights in the hold
Re-reading those last letters, scrambling up riggings,
Tacking sails, weathering out the storm.

Home on leave, he had fished the clipper from the fathoms
Of his new kit bag. Together they loaded
Their cargo of future, launched it down
The sideboard's slip on its maiden voyage.
And their star hung high, propitious, the night
They saw 'Gone with the Wind' at the Savoy
And, walking by the river, he promised, 'I'll be back!'
Her ship was scuppered by the telegram,
Her tall ship swapped for his ration of Players Weights.
It's how I know my father did not smoke.

'In My Father's House'

Fresh to 'the country', we clambered
Aboard the painted cart, bounced along
As Tom drove like a charioteer mistaking
Rutted roads for the Circus Maximus.

Between the field and our grandmother's cottage,
A path of fairy tale stepping stones as,
Shoes in hand, we felt the stream's *asperges*,
Danced the magic distance between worlds.

By the green half-door, she waited:
Delight on her lips, tears in her eye,
Her tremulous voice somewhere between
Gray's 'Elegy' and Schiller's 'Ode to Joy'.

Inside, the evocative smell and blush
Of turf under a kettle's soot-cosy
And the face of a bright full moon
Hanging from its nail on the wall.

The kitchen table was her theatre.
There she had kneaded flour, baked bread
For my father, lost to war, and the others
Blown by emigration like dandelion seeds.

I watched her milk the cow, head against haunch,
Relished the water-pistol hiss into the pail,
Heard 'spancel', another first, treasured
The silver sparkle of this newly minted word.

Chickens dined in pecking order. Geese cackled.
Like some maharaja on his howdah,
The blind cat hitched a lift on the collie's back
For her daily tour of the neighbouring fields.

Intrepid, we explored those fields and boreens,
The secrets behind bushes and dilapidated walls,
Ran barefoot with new friends seasoned
Against thistle, pine needle and thorn.

An adventure too far, I fell
Into a bog. The black wall offered no grip
As I slithered down, down into some dank hell,
All the way to above my knees,

Water so different from the wells and springs
Bottled, decades later, for export,
Like the one I brought to my mother, slithering
Down the cancer ward of the 'Royal Mineral'.

Everywhere the ripple of water, its score
Defying Mozart's quill. Beside a cousin's garden,
The river's versatile hymn had modified
From '*Puer Natus Est*' to '*Requiescat*'.

The parcel was an interlude, a treat
Between play: stamps, brown paper, string,
The blue contours of my aunt's handwriting,
The welcoming hand of bananas.

We took one to Tom in the field,
Tom who explained the mysteries of sickle
And scythe, whose arc and sweep cut rushes
Sparing the moist green croak of frogs.

At night he played the fiddle by the hearth.
When the taut string broke, it augured
That London day when he would snap,
When life would pluck him, *pizzicato*.

Night too was the haunt of Jack O'Lantern,
Leading astray those already shawled in darkness
Unless they turned their jackets inside out.
But who wore coats in summer?

No more than I did perched on a rock, casting
My hookless string into the two-inch stream,
My grandmother waving from the cottage door,
Her six-year-old son waving back.

Because we were children
It never rained that summer
When I learned to read the clock
But knew nothing about time.

A Sandstone Rock

It is hidden now, the sandstone rock,
Camouflaged by the khaki and boot polish
Of sally, hawthorn, screens of mountain ash:
The rock where a boy sat, haloed in sun,
Casting his hookless string in the two-inch
Dazzle of a stream, ambushing trout.

The thatched and whitewashed cottage is hidden too,
Its local stone returned to local earth,
The half-door sealed; some pharaoh's tomb:
The half-door where a woman watched the boy
As she had watched his father, six years old,
Perched on the same scorched rock with stick and string.

You will find him still among stones. Follow
The buzz of flies through the uniform
And serried standing-to-attention headstones,
His name and serial number hidden
Among the chiselled pride of names and numbers
Whose mothers watched them play from open doors.

Among The Rhododendrons

We walked among the rhododendrons,
Stepped lightly over gravel and roots
Throwing tentative thoughts like grappling hooks
To scramble aboard the world.

I scan their faces in the photograph,
Wonder to what shore the paths diverged
And how feathered time has flown
Swift as a swallow through the meadhall,

Conjecture the migrations of feet and mind,
The *'ubi sunt?'*. How distant now
That *terra firma* reef, the splintered sun,
The bright bees humming their spirituals.

Riverbank

What better place to open your account?
Current, of course, the interest rate
Phenomenal. And no time-lock vaults,
Just the Matisse wheeling of seasons

Holding hands in the ritual dance
Of alders alternating with the willows,
The sway of the rushes' Hawaiian hips,
The damselflies' bottle-green hum.

Perhaps the pike's sprung jaws lie lurking
In the shallows, but I see full quivers
Of water arrowheads, a border collie
Licking its reflection from the river,

The single waterhen zig-zagging
Through a maze of lily pads,
Frantic clouds of midges rearranging
Shapes like playful molecules.

Seven cygnets bob like paper boats
In the silver slipstream of a swan
And, casting their shadow on a passing
Trout, the heron's chasuble wings.

Local Anaesthetic

To alleviate the pain,
Gently apply the smell of cut grass
Or the cocktail scent
Wafting from the meadow,

Swallow the bark of a distant dog,
The thrush's speckled alleluia,
The hum of bees burgling
Colour from the lavender,

Sip a teaspoonful
Of sunset's purples and reds,
Of daisies winking
Through cracks in the pavement,

After dark, pull back the curtains
And watch gondola cloud pass
Across the moon. This dispensary
Is open day and night.

Seven Wonders Of The Parish

Daisies swivel towards the sun,
And buttercups
Button the field's greatcoat.

Outside a cottage door,
The stream's contralto
Scales six stepping stones.

Downstream, a speckled leap of trout
Freezes in mid-air,
Its ringed splash swimming towards the shore

Where a flicker of vixen
And her cubs
Ignites the broken wall.

Across the evening's quilted hills,
A quiet migration
Of low-flying cloud.

Later, the sequinned stars' reflections
Tango
On the river's polished floor.

And sometimes, on fresh snow, the record
Of a sparrow's journey
Printed in fluent Japanese.

Lady River

(paean to the Shannon)

Lady river, you know that I have always
Loved you, even when we played as children
And my doggy-paddle splashes tickled
Your toes.
            And I thought I was still playing
When you were Veronica, teasing
With that first puppy-love kiss.
You may remember I almost drowned,
Going down five times though I knew the limit
Was three. But you rejected me, aware
That I was way too young.
                Later we had
The best of each other, my freestyle strokes
Rippling across your silver skin from bank
To summer bank, my pike and swallow dives
Plunging, from high on the Tail-Race rocks,
Into your mysteries.
             These ebbing muscles
Are now no match for you, forever young,
Renewing yourself twice daily.
                And still
You tease. I watch you at high tide, demure,
Swan patterns embroidered on your evening
Dress, the stars stitching their sequins.
At low tide, your see-through nightie is flecked
With pure white lace.
             Whatever the tide,
You flow as beautiful as ever,
As dangerous, as irresistible.

Sunset On The Shannon

So little time that now
There is time
To admire the eternal
Variation of clouds, prompting
Responses we think we compose,

Inkblot clouds mirrored
On the Shannon,
Those precious rags,
Each with its restless geometry.

Tonight's is an apparition sky,
Silver rays
Dispensing blessings
And a golden brush flecking,
Tingeing the clouds' outlines

As if some child god
Was practising creation
And determined
His world would be beautiful.

Forecast

Morning will be bright
As the lark intoning lauds
From Kelly's hawthorn.

The day will vary,
Much like yesterday,
With hail showers
Like O'Brien's news from London
Darkening the Shannon.

Cloud will quilt across
Clare's capricious hills,
Some light as Mrs. Ryan's lumbago,

Some heavy as the Costello twins
Squeezing hands
At their mother's funeral.

Patches of intermittent love
Will linger in the afternoon.
This could be prolonged
For Jack and Pauline.

Evening's sun,
Though almost out of ink,
Will scribble its blessing
Across thatch and slate.

Night will draw in early,
Black
As the widow Casey's shawl.

As for tomorrow,
Prevailing winds would indicate
That tomorrow stays much the same.

Sidewinder

Sitting a safe distance
        From the TV screen,
You watched the sidewinder's
        Hilarious dance
Scribbling its one letter
        Alphabet in wonky
Parallels across
        The griddle of sand,
Dry waves starting
        From nowhere and ending
In the shelter of a shrub.

And watching the dance
        Of surprise in your eyes,
The joy in your waves
        Of laughter breaking
With spontaneous delight,
        I imagined the letters
Of love's alphabet
        Immeasurable as the stars
On a cloudless night.
        Raindrops tapped on the window
Seeking shelter from themselves.

Zebra Finch

I wanted a tour of her heart and mind;
She offered a tour of the house,

Walked me through warmly wallpapered rooms
And up the spiral stairway to high
White ceilings and oak-beamed bedrooms,
The blue one waiting for her daughter's return.

I listened to the history of the crystal chandelier,
The china jug and Fassett needlepoint,
Admired the rugs, a painting's Tuscan sky,
Her tennis cup, the settee's distressed finish.

The garden view leapfrogged fields and hedges
All the way to the sepia horizon.
I still recall the aviary's kaleidoscopic birds,
The keyboard feathers of the zebra finch,

Still read the shadows and reflections,
Hold each negative up to the light.

Not Being There

I still remember you not being there
That August at the chapel's wrought-iron gate
When the birds' *schola cantorum* intoned vespers
And my role was to check the time and wait.

We planned to walk by Guinness's canal,
Content to be together in the sun.
But I learned on that solitary stroll
That ultimately each one walks alone.

Your mother unexpectedly took ill
And there was no way you could let me know
That evening when our paths diverged, and still
I see the bulrushes, the dusty stones.

This time it's not your mother who is unwell,
And the pallbearers are always punctual.

Losing His Grip

Today his world is flat
And he lies flat
At the edge of the cliff,
Stretched taut,
Tortured on the rack

Of her slipping away,
Fingers losing their grip
And her frantic
Feet dangling
Like a hanged man's,

One shoe fallen
On the rocks below.
Nothing hurts more
Than this holding on,
Nothing, except the letting go.

A Seasonal Migration

Such casual ornithologists.
Unburdened by canvas and binoculars,
We spotted the unusual plumage,
Noted the unfamiliar song,
Giggled at the slight embarrassment
Of the visiting Yank in church
Or the aunt across from London
Who had 'lost the habit':
Their late standing for the gospel,
The way they pronounced 'Amen'.

The girl in the café reminded me,
The girl on her seasonal migration
Guided by a childhood star
And the tango of Christmas lights,
The girl in smart designer coat
Not yet stocked in the local shops,
In shoes not best for the rain,
Perched among friends, their chatter
An evening chorus, her song a fraction
Of a semi-tone out of key.

Changing Their Tune

The fox is altering its bark,
The urban fox, its habitat disturbed
By legislators' chainsaws
And developers' heavy plant.

Adventuring its run to the margins
Of our world, its cry has changed,
Roughed from that soft, rural bark
To the hoarse iambic of a loud moan
Followed by a shriek. The ghost
Of Darwin rubs his hairless hands.

Pioneer tits scout the city,
Announce their patch with a new,
High-pitched, staccato song
While their country cousins perpetuate
That long, slow, visceral twitter.

And, deceived by artificial lights,
Cantor robins intone the dawn chorus
A fraction of a note too soon,
Some chirping through the night
Since the day's high decibels
Drown their repertoire.

I know those interloping years
Spent sculpting vowels,
Chiselling at consonants.

I know that place
Where one single robin
Sings only at night.

A Candle In The Window

The Christmas candle was a low star
Over Bethlehem. Every year the ritual:
His father lighting the candle, his mother
Placing it – red as a stick of seaside
Rock – in the kitchen window,
A glow to cheer neighbour and passerby.
Each household shone its part
In this glittering constellation.

Later, in Dublin's Phoenix Park,
The President touched her taper
To the burning memory of hunger years
When the starving built the famine roads
That led only to exile or a pauper's grave,
And placed her candle, memorial and beacon
For the diaspora, in the kitchen window
Of *Aras an Uachtarain*.

That broken road to exile was well worn
By generations, reviving *spalpeen* days,
Waiting for the ganger at London's bleak
Street corners. By day the rhythm of shovel
And pick, then the rhythm of *ceili* and the *craic*
To deafen the long night's loneliness.
One a friend, invisible and spent,
Prisoner of the wheelchair and the couch.

Now gangrene spreads its metaphor,
Drips down his skeletal legs
Like congealed wax on candles.
His own wick flickers, too far across
The years to see the candles in the town,
Too far across the miles to recognise
The symbol, vigilant in the window
Of *Aras an Uachtarain*.

A Prayer In Search Of Its God

The prayer circled granite boulders,
Danced around the maypole,
Watched incense rise from the stream.

Buckling its sandals, it took
A compass reading for the sacred
Confluence of the Jumna and the Ganges.

In dispersed synagogues, it listened
To commandments chiselled on stone,
Heard the plaintive 'Next year in Jerusalem'.

Following the Eightfold Path to Enlightenment,
It entered temples and pagodas,
Sat beneath the fig tree in Bodh Gaya.

Scaling the backs of holy mountains,
It listened to ancestral voices
And the wind's conversation in the trees

Before tracing the Nazarene's steps,
Following miracles and parables
To another tree on Golgotha.

Facing Mecca, it unrolled its mat
Then set out for Mount Hira
Where Gabriel appeared to the prophet.

And, at the Cathedral of the Pines, witnessed
The green carpet spread its welcome
Before every religion and belief.

Maleficium

Women who survived the ducking stool
Were manifestly guilty. How else
Defy the fetid pond, the weeds'
Crone fingers clawing at their face?

Hounded by the charge of '*maleficium*',
Lacerated knees and feet were dragged
Across the stony ground, the trail
Marking another Via Dolorosa.

Then the tying to the splintered stake,
Her pleas for mercy scorched by the inferno,
Its thousand crimson, taunting tongues
Insatiable, licking into flesh.

Sometimes they tossed familiars – dogs, cats,
Hyenas, owls, baboons – to swell the pyre.
Poking through the ashes of Saint Joan,
They found her heart, that and the femur of a cat.

Centuries outside lace curtains
And Venetian blinds, a splash beneath the bridge
Disturbs the night; the air is tortured
With the creak of gallows, the crackle of skin.

Would we have found someone to blame
If milk had curdled or the cow not calved?
Would we have pointed at some girl
Because the brown hen had not laid since Tuesday?

The Minus Decibels

Something like a hazel rod twitches
Searching for silence, knows it is more
Than the absence of noise. Silence hides, wrapped
In that moment before the lark's first note,
Between the lead violin's fine tuning
And the maestro raising his baton.
It shifts roadblocks between the cowled monk
And his heaven, falls soft as soot and the velvet
Curtain of night. Visible, it would be
Churchbells drifting across Christmas snow.
Its breaking is a Ming vase dropped
In the whispering gallery.
Its aim, to spread its muffled carpet
Under the unfathomable feet
Of something deeper than silence.

Horae Canonicae

Matins

Not a chorister, the nightingale's
Solo calls from brambles
To the midnight sky.

*

Imagine life in a single day,
Beginning with a discreet whisper
And the flutter of an angel's wing.

Lauds

Like monks in the choir stalls,
The lark on his perch
Sings canticles of praise.

*

A mother sings a lullaby,
Rocks her newborn baby
In arms soft as feathers.

Prime

A blackbird hops on the lawn,
First light catching
His gold medal beak for singing.

*

The child takes huge
Himalayan steps, toddles
After meadow butterflies.

Terce

Perched on the garden rockery,
A songthrush mimics other birds,
Perfects its speckled repertoire.

*

Stepping out from childhood,
The boy surfs hormones,
Scans for elusive love.

Sext

The robin's metallic tick tick
Echoes an analogue watch;
Its breast reflects the sun.

*

Invincible, the young man
Climbs his mountains,
Swims his turbulent seas.

Nones

Sparrows are familiars, shadow us,
Repeat chirps and chiddicks
To a rosary of song.

*

Unlike birds, the man
Has learned to labour and to spin,
Builds his nest of stone.

Vespers

The sun dips its toe
In the sea. Evening
Is a murmuration of starlings.

*

Time collects its toll. Muscles
Lose their desire to row.
The horizon not so distant now.

Compline

An owl breaks cover from the barn,
Its white, ghost music
Calling somebody's name.

*

The old man whispers his last
Words, folds into night.
Nothing like a dying swan.

The Canonical Hours
Matins: Midnight/Daybreak
Lauds: First of Day Hours
Prime: Sunrise, 6 a.m.
Terce: Third Hour, 9 a.m.
Sext: Sixth Hour, Noon
Nones: Ninth Hour, 3 p.m.
Vespers: Evening
Compline: Last Hour

Her Christmas Card List

The handwriting impeccable,
Her litany of names inscribed
In fluent, blue biro,
Trademark elegant 'M's fluttering
Across pages like ribbons
On Christmas parcels.
So before the arthritis set in.

In pride of place, the pedestalled
Familial names, her neat
Amendments landmarks to dispersal,
The crossings-out confirming each demise.

Next, the dwindling bunch
Of oldest friends,
Flowers from the same spring garden.

The unfamiliar ones are stones
Across a stream, paths
To that vast and guessable world,
To doors without a latchkey for the kids.

And, beside each name,
A careful tick,
Limping slightly
In the latter years.

But no mention of the sister
Who left home at seventeen
Or the other, younger son,
The one who was adopted.

Taking Down The Decorations

She waits for the Epiphany
Before taking them down,
The same decorations as last year
And the year before,

The same tinsel and streamers
That every year are just a little
Further out of reach, the box
A little heavier to carry.

She packs them carefully away,
Remembers when he brought
Each bauble home, each paper bell,
The glittering strata of a life.

She pours another cup of tea,
Rereads the Christmas cards
From daughter and three sons,
Cards that arrive each year with foreign stamps.

Raspberry Ripple

Compelled by its Svengali call,
The widows in their cardies and soft slippers
Flutter 'round the ice-cream van,
Taste buds sharp as in those pigtail summers
Racing to the flavoured chimes.

Faded now the jostling boys,
The chatter of wedding bells.
And when the village clock strikes three
They know the hour is accurate;
It is the year they can't believe.

Returning to neat bungalows,
Memories tango and fox-trot,
Ripple through the vanilla afternoon.
Some, like the silent '*p*'
In raspberry, deliciously discreet.

Watching Agatha What'shername

She has settled in well
Since leaving her purse and memory
On the back seat of the 24 bus

And seems happy,
Or not aware of being unhappy
Which comes to much the same.

Visitors resembling
The photos on her dressing table
Are sure of a smile,

Especially that man
Beside the girl in white dress and white veil
Clutching a bouquet of May flowers.

Now, sitting on the garden bench,
Her head still pivots
Like a daisy towards the sun.

And she picks the long night's lock
With her pink crochet needle,
Watches re-runs of whodunnits

But never remembers who did.
Her favourites star Miss Marple
In the Agatha What'shernames.

Here she sinks
In the cocoa and cardigan comfort
Of cottages framing the village green,

Cream teas on the manor lawn,
The dactyl huff
Of the 4.50 from Paddington,

A flicker of vicarage roses
Fresh as the flowers the man in the photo
Brings every Sunday afternoon.

The Invisible Man

There are clues in the gradient ratio,
Its steep change on the morning hill,

And in the way the walk to town
Is surreptitiously longer,

Clues too in the bent reflection
Taunting from shop front and car window,

In shadows that had kept in step
Now lingering in the latter years,

In winter's frostier snap and bite,
And being invisible at street corners

Where he looked cool in blue suede shoes –
Bone comb in back pocket.

The clues are gathering and gathering speed,
Rolling with the gradient downhill.

Allegro

(for Fred)

It was not as if life was lived
In a minor key. The anecdotes
And stories were proof that it was full
As champagne glasses raised
In toasts at his birthday bash,

Though he himself recalled the dealer
Slipping that card from underneath the deck
When piano keys were key to his future
And the great depression's knuckles
Knocked, importunate at the door.

No, the years were not metronome years.
The worst of times, with swagbag and mask,
Did not burgle his music. It was there
In *fortissimo* handshakes, *vivace* eyes,
In fingers hurting for *allegro* keys.

Jigsaw Man

The jigsaw man sat on the broken wall
'Cutting his smoke' (his quarter moon
Plug tobacco, Mick McQuaid), cupping
A hand around the pipe's briar bowl
To shield the flickering match against the breeze.

But the jigsaw man is not quite what is painted
On the box. A few pieces are missing:
The gap left when his son just disappeared
At seventeen; when, one by one, his other
Son and daughters 'took the boat' steered

By the star that promised a weekly wage;
And when his wife asked *sotto voce* for the sip
Of water (echoes of Golgotha)
That proved to be her last – slid pieces not
Retrieved by searching down the sofa's side.

Evening whistled high through the jigsaw man
Sitting on the broken wall, rehearsed
A *cante jondo* repertoire. But only
The wall was broken. So many other
Pieces holding him together: the fireside

Songs and stories, those riverside walks,
That interval of children prancing
Like spring lambs, his granddaughter's electric
Smile – defiant embers around which he cupped
His weathered hands, this keeper of the flame.

The Final Credits

Slowly, the credits climb
Like tired smoke towards the ceiling,
The lead roles played
By mother, father, family, friends.

Supporting cast (also
Deserving oscars), key grip, best boy,
Rigging gaffer and director are dismantled
Like some scaffolding 'round a life.

Theme music fades. Already,
The last frame ebbs to memory.
Scenes dissipate. 'Indelible'
Images leak their dye.

The lights go on. The theatre empties.
The national anthem does not play.

Drawn Thread Embroidery

(for Ilda on her ninetieth birthday)

She sits at her embroidery,
Fingers deft as when they danced
Across piano keys or pressed
The solemn organ stops
At St. John Vianney's.

Her embroidery is 'drawn thread'.
Patiently, she picks each one
As if drawing on the warp and weft,
The days, the nights, the fabric
Of her life, towards something

Intricate and beautiful.
Maybe it will portray a rose,
A butterfly, a bird. Perhaps
The flying jewel, the daylight star
Of an iridescent sunbird.

For certain, if it is a bird,
We know that it will sing.

The Everyday Aesthetic

Beside ubiquitous nettles grow
The dockleaves of the everyday aesthetic.

No need to journey to some Grand Canyon
Or Taj Mahal, or join a winding
Queue for Van Gogh, Titian, Velasquez.
And no admission fee to view
A dewdrop studding the thistle's ear
Or swarms of stars jewelling the night,
To hear a thrush rehearse his speckled scales
Above the shallow whisper of a stream.
How would Christie's expert frame
And what reserve price would he set
For the buttercups and daisies
Periscoping in a cobbled yard?

Is there a hurt that a rainbow leap
Of trout will not bandage?

This Hillside Rock

Earth groins rock in her vast
Maternity ward, coughs up
Stones like smokers' phlegm
On a winter morning,

Stones of all sizes:
Pebbles that a lover
Might toss at a window
Or the scruple in a pilgrim's shoe,

A bigger one for David's sling
And bigger still to cast
At Stephen while Saul
Guarded the coats.

Some stones claim their landscape
Like circles by a leyline,
Stonehenge's monoliths,
The Burren's dolmen shaped like pi.

And what of this hillside rock
With its clumsy heart and initials
Recording the indelible springtime
Of a perfect love,

This patient rock unmoved
Since the last ice age?
Perhaps the rains have scrubbed
The blood of human sacrifice

Or was it a mass rock
In penal days, witness
To Latinate prayer and a fear
That silenced the Sanctus bell?

Would a passing Michelangelo
Envisage its perfect form
Or lend his chisel
To the prevailing wind?

Bard

'they love the dead, the living man they hate'
(*'**The Poet Down**', Michael Hartnett*)

We met on a summer morning
In Limerick's People's Park:
Me, searching under your flowerpot words
For the key to poetry,
You, spread with a hawk's wingspan
Between the covers of '*A Farewell to English*'.

A temporary parting. You returned,
Seamlessly soldered the links of the broken chain.

Your friendships were stronger than chains,
And your flocks of poems soared,
Lyrics to the song of blackbird
And thrush. The plaudits rained.

Too soon the seepage of spirits and stout
Swelled to a drowning tide.
Too soon the
        'Four hounds gone south,
        one with your liver in his mouth'.

Now the monument, the Eigse
In the town you left
'To escape the mundane',
The prayers for your winged soul
In the church where Christ
Carries His cross walking backwards,
The glasses raised to your memory
In every pub from which you were barred.

The Salon Of The Refused

Cezanne, Pissarro, Fantin-Latour,
Whistler, Manet with his scandalous
Le Dejeuner sur l'Herbe.
Rejected by the Academie,

They, in turn, reject the jurors,
Fling open the welcoming doors
Of the *Salon de Refuses*
Wide as an eagle's golden span.

Word gets around, coaxes
In from the window ledge,
Down from the bedroom's makeshift gallows,
Flushes tablets down the loo.

A lengthening procession joins
The queue: hope renewed, blueprints
For beauty, peace and love folded
Like canvases underneath the arm.

About *Le Dejeuner,* notice
The hint of Giorgione,
The echo of Raphael,
The paint still wet.

Harp

Scion of the twang of a hunter's bow,
The harp is the voice of water
Trickling over stones,
Best friend to the human voice,
Partner in mining emotions' motherlodes.

Plato thought it inferior
To the lyre.
But what did he know,
A man who would banish the poets?

Poets like David who strummed it
As he hymned his psalms.

Its soundboard resonated
From Egypt's scorched sands
To Greece's stone monuments,
Echoed through the palace halls
Of Tara and Versailles.

Shapeshifting from arch and trigonon
And curved forepillar,
Aways the beauty queen of instruments.

Versatile, it voiced war anthems
And the fervent lyrics of love.

Classical, it sang Beethoven's Prometheus,
The Orpheus of Hayden,
Berlioz' Symphonie Fantastique.

Intimate, Carolan shouldered his harp
Between the stations of poor parishes;
Its willow still weeps on emigrant quays.

What more poignant image
Than a harp with broken strings?
What better symbol of hope
Than a broken harp repaired?

Strung between earth and the heavens,
In tune with both,
It welcomes Aeolian fingers.

Small wonder the wind
Does not cut its nails.

Lifebuoy

Absorbed by the Shannon,
Standing between birch trees
With leaves falling like golden arrowheads
And a stout stone wall
Not prey to the gales,
I watched the river sedately flow
Under the seven arches of Thomond Bridge
Then gather speed like an athlete
Before the leap to join the discreet
Curragower falls, its thousand churnings
White as childhood's whipped ice-creams.

To conjure a more perfect time
Would be disloyal to the moment.
Bernini could have sculpted me
With an arrow in my heart.

A wagtail perched beside me,
Its flickering tail a finger beckoning,
Admonishing me to cherish, take note
For days when the clouds might gather.

What I noted was the lifebuoy,
Reminder of those other leaps,
The ice-cream days forgotten,
A lifebuoy perched in a yellow box
Like a vigilant mother leaning
Across a half-door, the yellow
Not quite rhyming with the arrowheads.
Written on the box, the legend:
'A Stolen Ringbuoy – A Stolen Life'.
And, circled in the bullseye
Centre of the buoy:
'Samaritans 1850-60-90-90
You don't have to be alone.'

Interrupting Children's Hour

(Munich: 3.04 p.m., Thursday 6th February 1958)

Their names are written on Munich snow:
Geoff Bent, Roger Byrne, Eddie Coleman, Duncan Edwards,
Mark Jones, David Pegg, Tommy Taylor, Billy Whelan,
Names that gatecrashed eternity
Through the airport's perimeter fence
And interrupted Children's Hour
On the BBC and playing fields everywhere.

Still they play the beautiful game
With never a word of protest to the Ref.
Who blew His whistle too early.
On clear nights, you can see them shimmer,
The Busby galaxy, passing, moving, shooting,
And Frank Swift plucking
Their comets from the Salford sky.

Last Minute Packing

He had no need for slaves or concubines,
Pyramids pointing to propitious stars,
Armies for some terracotta war,
Torcs, broadsword, a hoard of golden coins;
And no wish to be laid out in a brown
Franciscan robe with dog-tag scapulars,
No copper pennies on his eyes – full fare
Demanded by the shrouded ferryman.
Instead, he chose, folded and packed the memory
Of waking to a dream of Christmas stockings,
Holding his mother's hand against the hill,
The thrush's speckled lauds on the rockery,
That slow kiss at the bus stop in the rain,
Such treasures as tomb raiders cannot steal.

Counting The Seconds

The gods were just being playful
In their wanton way,
Hurtling thunderbolts, with sound effects,
To scare the three-year-old.

We called their bluff.
Standing by the window,
She braved the cartoon sky
And we made a game

Of counting on tiny fingers
The seconds between flash and thunder clap,
Watched the burden of fear soon melt
Like a sack of salt in water.

But the gods were not at play
When the Citroen skidded on black ice
And shot like lightning across the country road,
Targeting her bicycle.

Split-screen memories compete.
Again, I stand by the window
Holding her abacus hand, counting
The seconds, those precious seconds.

Sundial

Cannock's clock struck
Every quarter hour
And, round the corner
At the Central and Savoy,
Consumptive heroines
Were dying in black and white.

Soon the Wurlitzer
Disappearing from the pit,
The novelty of talkies,
Colour and wide screen,
The art house movies,
Subtitled.

In the streets outside,
Children play in cinemascope
And glorious technicolour,
CCTV cameras proliferate,
Ubiquitous the Babel babble
Of mobile 'phones.

Church bells chime, announce
The wedding of today and yesteryear.
Confetti emulates the rain.
For better or worse,
All parties agree there is
No turning back the sundial.

The Landlord's Daughter

(Connemara, circa 1847)

Those master masons, the house martins,
Were busy in the eaves, compacting mud,
Trowelling with practised beaks,
Lining the nest with grass and feathers,
Faithful to the blueprint of their DNA.

The swoop and glide of their aerial display
Caught the eye of the landlord's daughter.

Then came bailiff and wrecking ball,
The dance of light on bayonet and sword,
The torched thatch, its crackling reds competing
With the sizzle of a setting sun.

They say she cried, the landlord's daughter,
On hearing the house martins were dislodged.
And before the eggs were hatched.

1888

1888, and the blazing guns
Of Wyatt Earp were still creating
Myths and legends of the West.

Back East, more subtle
Than range war cutters and lassoes,
Edison's inventions were tearing down fences

And, in St. Louis, Missouri,
The Eliot bird hatched and sang
An entirely original song.

Van Gogh's brush was frantic in Arles,
Daubing boots and stars, planting sunflowers
On a raw and brilliant canvas

While Faure's legato soared above Paris,
The '*Pie Jesu*' and '*In Paradisum*'
Jewelling his immortal Requiem.

Rising from phosphorus fumes,
The striking Match Girls of London's Bow
Were more than a match for Bryant and May

And, cloaked in Whitechapel's midnight fog,
Some scalpel-wielding nobody
Was disembowelling young women.

That too was deemed of historical note
In the year my grandfather was born,
Discreet as the Maigue rippling through Adare

But of note to me, my tangible root,
Hardy as briar and oak. Before that,
A paper chase history, an origami family tree

With his parents' faint names penned
In the parish register. And his parents' parents
Who survived the Hunger of '45.

Proclamations, 1916

('If we do nothing else, we will rid Ireland of three bad poets.'
Padraic Pearse, early spring 1916)

Pearse, MacDonagh, Plunkett.
History encases them in bronze,
This flesh and blood trinity of poets.

We commemorate their deeds,
Their public words echoing
From the steps of Dublin's G.P.O.,
Subtitles to the rifles' rattle,
The rubble, the Liffey on fire.

Outside history, we celebrate
The intimate proclamations of their poems,
Their eastering lyrics.

One anguished at the passing
Of 'a red lady-bird upon a stalk'.
Another innocently looked 'with Adam's eyes
In the first days of Paradise'.
The youngest saw Christ's blood
Crimson on the rose
And 'God's high glory
In a girl's soft shape'.

Each hymned the universe.
And each penned the last full stop
On his very last poem, knowing
It was final as a bullet.

In The Valley Of The Thrushes

That first morning when Oisin rode out
From the pages of our new class reader
To gallop on the great white horse
Across the waves of the western sea
With Princess Niamh riding pillion,
We followed on magical stepping-stone
Words to the land of Tir na n-Og
Where the sun never set and the rain never fell
And the small birds never stopped singing.

When the salt breeze ferried thoughts of home
And Oisin's lungs hurt for the hunt of the elk by day,
For the campfire's warrior songs by night,
I knew that salmon feeling, that restless something
At the bend of the river insisting on return.

When, back among familiar streams and hills,
He saw the Fianna fortresses in ruins,
Scabbed with nettles, brambles, briars . . . ,
I took the airport bus to town and saw
The glass and concrete canyons of supermarkets
And hotels, the churches, emptied of their choirs,
In the unjoined hands of entrepreneurs.

And when, in the Valley of the Thrushes,
Lifting the stone too heavy for sixteen men,
The saddle girth snapped and he toppled to earth
Like a felled and withering oak,
The music I heard was the song of Fionnuala.
A night breeze turns the final pages. The book slips
Softly as feathers falling from the children of Lir.

*Poetry is like bread, it should be shared by all, by scholars and
by peasants, by all our vast, incredible, extraordinary family of humanity.*

Pablo Neruda

Revival Press is the poetry imprint of The Limerick Writers' Centre.

It was founded in 2007 by Dominic Taylor, who is managing editor.

It grew out of the Revival Poetry Readings established in Limerick 2003

by Barney Sheehan and Dominic Taylor.

It has published twenty eight titles to date including three anthologies.

Their most popular anthology has been *I Live in Michael Hartnett,*

an anthology of poems written in tribute to the late County Limerick poet.

Revival has also helped establish a number of local and national poets

by publishing their first collections.

One of the aims of Revival Press is to revive

the long tradition of book publishing in Limerick, especially poetry books.

It continues to represent local authors

and to offer advice and encouragement to aspiring writers.